FASHION IN THE TIME OF WILLIAM SHAKESPEARE

Sarah Jane Downing

Published in Great Britain in 2014 by Shire Publications Ltd, PO Box 883, Oxford, OX1 9PL, UK.

PO Box 3985, New York, NY 10185-3985, USA.

E-mail: shire@shirebooks.co.uk
www.shirebooks.co.uk

A CIP catalogue record for this book is available from the British Library.

Shire Library no. 785.   ISBN-13: 978 0 74781 354 5

PDF e-book ISBN: 9781784420130

ePub ISBN: 9781784420123

Sarah Jane Downing has asserted her right under the Copyright, Designs and Patents Act, 1988, to be identified as the author of this book.

Designed by Tony Truscott Designs, Sussex, UK and typeset in Garamond Pro and Gill Sans.

Printed in China through Worldprint Ltd.

14 15 16 17 18   10 9 8 7 6 5 4 3 2 1

COVER IMAGE
Robert Dudley, 1st Earl of Leicester (1532–88), *c.* 1560s (oil on panel by Steven van der Meulen). (Yale Center for British Art, Paul Mellon Collection, USA / Bridgeman Images)

TITLE PAGE IMAGE
Lady with a Fleur-de-Lys Jewel (Nicholas Hilliard *c.* 1595). The lady, once thought to be Ann, Countess of Dorset, is wearing court costume.

CONTENTS PAGE IMAGE
Detail of image on page 45.

ACKNOWLEDGEMENTS
My heartfelt thanks to my parents, to David, Sacha, and especially my sister Emma who gave me the inspiration. Thanks also to the fabulous people at Shire, particularly Russell Butcher who has been with me at every step.

Image copyright is acknowledged as follows:

Ashmolean Museum, University of Oxford, UK/ Bridgeman Art Library, page 56; Bridgeman Art Library, page 20 and 62; Lord Daventry, Arbury Hall, Warwickshire, page 46; Hardwick Hall, Derbyshire, UK/National Trust Photographic Library/P. A. Burton/Bridgeman Art Library, page 12; Hardwick Hall, Derbyshire, UK/National Trust Photographic Library/John Hammond/Bridgeman Art Library, page 33; Hatfield House, Hertfordshire, UK/Bridgeman Art Library, page 4; National Portrait Gallery, pages 36 and 44; Tate Images, page 26; Shakespeare's Birthplace Trust, page 53; Victoria and Albert Museum, London, pages 52 and 60; Wallace Collection, London, UK/ Bridgeman Art Library, page 31.

All other images are from the Author's collection.

CONTENTS

WOOL, GLORIOUS WOOL

S HAKESPEARE BELIEVED THAT 'clothes maketh the man' and dressed his characters accordingly using costume not only to denote character, but also to drive plot through subterfuge and disguise, notably through cross-dressing. Garments and fashions feature in almost all of his plays, occasionally even as the pivot of the story, as with Malvolio's stockings in *Twelfth Night*, the handkerchief in *Othello* and the sleeve given as a love token in *Troilus and Cressida*.

Shakespeare extensively explored what could happen if the strict rules of dress were transgressed, from the potentially serious consequences of violating the social contract, to the folly of individual vanity. He raises more than a smile when characters cross-dress, opening up issues of identity and sexuality at a time long before individual expression was considered important.

Shakespeare's use of disguising women as improbable pageboys seems rather clumsy to the twenty-first-century eye but in the late sixteenth century it was a popular dramatic device that had quite a different resonance. There was a curious frisson of seeing a young crack-voiced boy playing a girl who was pretending to be a young man, which would have been enjoyed by theatregoers as much as farcical humour. Fashionable young men of the time delighted in all kinds of finery and made themselves look quite effeminate, to the disgust of conservative commentators – as Shakespeare described, like the 'hawthorne buds' that pranced around court – and it was not too much of a

Opposite:
A Fête at Bermondsey (Joris Hoefnagel, c. 1570). It was important to Elizabethans to be able instantly to assess others by their dress, placing them in their idea of the 'natural order'.

Moralists like Philip Stubbes were deeply upset by women adopting male styles, describing them as 'stinkyng before the face of god and offensive to man'.

theatrical stretch for a woman to be convincingly disguised as a handsome young man.

Elizabethans were used to finding amusement in role exchange since it was a popular element of festivities each Christmas, introduced by the Lord of Misrule. Most often it consisted of a lowly servant exchanging roles with a lord, but from the 1580s on there are reports of women exchanging clothes with husbands or brothers that were written of with bitter disapproval by Puritan commentators. Unsettled by the 'unnaturalness' of a female monarch, they held a deep-seated fear that women who adopted breeches under their skirts for riding or wore masculine styles of doublet or hat would be tempted away from their rigidly defined female role into immoral freedom. Mary Fitton, one of the Queen's ladies-in-waiting, caused outrage when she slipped out at night to meet her lover disguised in a man's cloak with her skirts tucked up in a most unseemly manner to mount her horse; the misuse of cloak and skirt were almost a greater scandal than the lover!

Such excitement was strictly for the silk-brocaded classes; for the rest it was wool, from the finest worsteds down to itchy homespun. Wool was at the heart of the economy, so much so that the Lord Chancellor's seat of power in Parliament was upon a woolsack sent by wool merchants as a reminder of their place as the backbone of English wealth. It was the need and desire to establish new markets for English wool in the 1560s that encouraged daring entrepreneurs to travel to mysterious lands such as Persia, Russia, West Africa, Morocco and the Americas. They established trade links and enriched the kingdom with territories such as Virginia and newly discovered commodities of potatoes, tobacco and cotton, while laying the groundwork for England to rule the waves. Sadly it was also the birth of Britain's participation in the slave trade.

If wool was the heart of the economy, then fashion was its lifeblood, producing wealth and driving demand. No longer content to wait until their senior years to wear the furred finery of a Guild gown, the nouveau riche wanted to enjoy the silks and velvets imported from Venice, or exciting fabrics such as russels, darnick and tuff mockado that were newly

in production in England as part of the influx of Artisan Strangers. In many cases they had made their wealth on the back of England's millions of sheep, and a great number of their rank felt that it was an appalling betrayal to wear anything other than decent English wool.

Lord Mayor and Aldermen (Lucas van de Heere, c. 1566–71). Made in rich wool and fur-lined, the Guild gown was a status symbol that could be earned only by a lifetime of hard work.

In addition to running her home, a good wife of the lower orders would spin her own wool, weave it and use it to make clothes for her family.

Most people revelled in their disposable income and were desperate to wear the finest their money could buy – from glamorous gilded rebatos and fans down to the silkiest peach stockings – even if that meant breaking the law. Sumptuary laws that dictated what each social class was allowed to wear were relaxed somewhat from earlier reigns, but still issued periodically between 1559 and 1597. Some were clearly defined to promote English industry over

The Shepherdess (woodcut, c. 1580), adheres to sumptuary law – if not its spirit – so long as she makes her gown from wool and keeps her ruff suitably small.

Figures derived from Hoefnagel's map of Nonsuch Palace (c. 1574). The countrywoman is marked by her chin clout worn to protect from dust while travelling, but even she wears a ruff.

foreign imports, but most were aimed at maintaining class order.

Fashion was a political issue, as a matter set in law, allowing luxury for some and debarring others. Many people felt that greed and social climbing were not only sins, but also seriously damaging to an economy rendered fragile by inflation. William Harrison in his *Description of England* … (1577) worried, 'Oh, how much cost is bestowed nowadays upon our bodies and how little upon our souls!'

Deeply concerned by the variety and 'confuse mingle mangle of apparell',

the Puritan writer Philip Stubbes felt that pride in dress was the greatest sin of all, as beautiful garments were 'the devilles nettes, to intangle poore soules in'. He despised the international muddle of fashion and the ungainly disloyal look it created, as did Harrison, who claimed 'except it were a dog in a doublet you shall not see any so disguised as are my countrymen of England'.

Where writers like Stubbes took a direct hectoring approach, producing reams of critical prose, Shakespeare used art and stagecraft to dress his observations in poetry and humour. He was in a better place than most to view society from multiple perspectives. During his childhood his own position had been undermined when his illustrious father, chief alderman and bailiff in Stratford-upon-Avon in 1568, was found to have been dealing illegally in wool and prosecuted for usury; he also foolishly lost William's inheritance. However, Shakespeare was able to use his talents and entrepreneurship to earn a place at court, performing for and rubbing shoulders with the most celebrated of his age while also raking in a handsome share of the profits from his theatre company, The Lord Chamberlain's Men. Inevitably there was some disapproval, and when he

In 1592 the Duke of Württemberg wrote: 'The women of England go dressed out in exceedingly fine clothes … whilst at home perhaps they have not a piece of dry bread.'

Fine dress worn by all classes is apparent in M. van Meer's *Album Amicorum*, 1614: top, the Lord Mayor of London; middle, the Lady Mayoress of London; bottom left, a citizen and his wife who appears to be busy spinning even while riding; bottom right, a peasant woman going to market.

New clothes were commissioned for special occasions; for a wedding trousseau, fine fabrics would be taken to the tailor along with existing clothes of the best fit to 'translate the pattern'.

renewed his father's application to the Office of Heraldry to be granted a coat of arms, there was a certain derision at 'Shakespear the player' thinking himself so grand; yet the fact that it was awarded when his father's application had been denied twenty-five years earlier is testament not only to personal achievement, but to the changing times that his literature had helped to form.

A *Christmas Play by Shakespeare Performed for Queen Elizabeth I*, engraved from the painting by Sir John Gilbert, c. 1858. Many of Shakespeare's plays were performed at court by his company, The Lord Chamberlain's Men.

QUEEN AND COURT

To see Elizabeth was to see England. She was the most spectacular person in the land, and her own greatest masterpiece. Just as her father had honed his vast presence into a legend bringing with it one of Europe's second-rate kingdoms, Elizabeth showed her 'weak and feeble body' to be transcendent when she shackled it to her country, making it glorious as she made herself Gloriana.

Her feminine leadership was deeply opposed from all sides, and for decades she had to make herself available on the marriage market as her advisors prayed for an alliance with a suitable prince. Walking the uneasy line between pretty potential bride and indomitable leader she styled herself to highlight her beautiful features and flatter the tastes of her prospective suitors.

Her vast official wardrobe was bursting with over 3,000 jewelled and richly embroidered gowns and no end of accessories, fans and wigs. Elizabeth carefully managed this collection, the treasures of which she considered to be state treasures as much as her own. A thoughtful stylist, she organised garments in combinations, not only to flatter and suit herself, but to display her vast wealth and the bounty of her ever-growing empire while also showing each visiting dignitary especial courtesy by wearing something reflecting his culture or one of his previous gifts.

Gloriana opened the Royal Exchange on 23 January 1570. Based on the concept of the 'Bourse' in Amsterdam it brought together a select group of milliners, haberdashers,

Opposite:
Portrait of Elizabeth I (Studio of Nicholas Hilliard, c. 1592). She wears a fore-part depicting the flora and fauna of her dominions. A description from the Wardrobe Accounts, c. 1600, records: '… embroidered all over with verie faire like seas, with dyvers devyses of rockes, shippes, and fishes, with venice golde, sylver, and garnished with some seed pearle'.

starchers and feather-dressers to offer the most luxurious celebration of fashion this side of Venice. The poet Nicholas Breton described the dazzling array of goods in *The Fort of Fancy* (1577):

Such purses, gloves and points
Of cost and fashion rare,
Such cutworks, partlets, suits of lawn,
Bongraces and such ware;

The Ditchley Portrait of Elizabeth I (Marcus Gheeraerts the Younger, 1592). The swell of the queen's silver and white gown was noted to be 'much greater than is the fashion in France'.

Such gorgets, sleeves and ruffs,
Linings for gowns and cauls,
Coifs, crippins, cornets, billaments,
Musk boxes and sweet balls;
Pincases, pick-tooths, beard-brushes,
Combs, needles, glasses, bells,
And many such like toys as these,
That gain to fancy sells.

Queen Elizabeth at Prayer from 'Queen Elizabeth's Prayerbook', 1569. John Aylmer wrote in 1559 that her maidenly apparel would have made noblemen's daughters and wives 'ashamed to be drest and paynted lyke pecockes'.

As the Puritans surely predicted, such wanton displays of tempting fripperies were bound to attract 'the wrong sort'. Swaggering through the throng came the gallants, keen to cut a dash and impress the ladies with, as Thomas Dekker describes, 'much casting open of cloaks to publish new clothes'. Aside from a break in the afternoon to visit the theatre, the gallants spent much of the day there, Bishop Hall describing in his *Satires* (1598) 'Tattelius, the new-come traveller, with his disguised coat and new-ringed ear tramping the Bourse's marble twice a day'.

The Royal Exchange was the most important shopping venue in Shakespeare's England.

Any provincial lady who found herself in London would head to the Exchange as soon as she had the chance. If ladies couldn't make the trip themselves, baffled husbands were dispatched with detailed descriptions of the perfect shade of 'maiden's blush' pink ribbon or 'lustie gallant' red feathers to buy, and woe betide them if they failed to

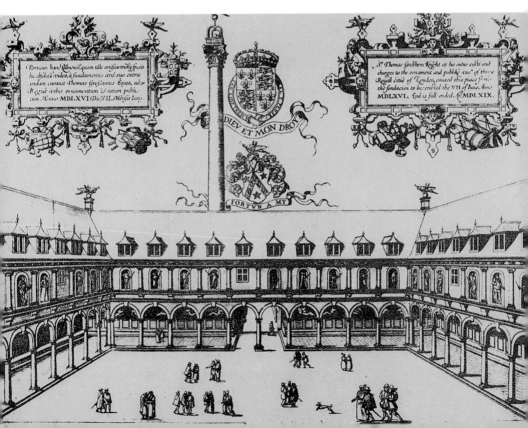

return with the correct articles together with a description of all the latest styles they had seen there.

When Philip Gawdy visited Elizabeth's court in 1587 his sisters – presumably still at home in his native Norfolk – were desperate for him to report every possible detail of the fashions he saw. Luckily he was able to reassure his sister Ann 'that bothe the queene and all the gentlewomen at the courte weare the very fashion of yor tuff taffeta gowne with an open wired sleeve and such a cutt, and it is now the newest fashion'. She was undoubtedly delighted to convey to all her friends, that she was as fashionably dressed as the Queen!

Once marriage talks petered out in 1582 and Elizabeth determined that she would rule alone she made sure that every item she wore and every portrait made of her would work to crystallise her image as Gloriana the Virgin Queen sacrificing herself for her nation and her people's love for her. Elizabeth frequently used the symbol of the pelican – known for pecking its own bosom to feed its young – as a reminder of this sacrifice. She also became more extravagant in her costume, employing voluminous styles to create a majestic presence and a huge surface area to be lavishly decorated with a rich symbolism, reinforcing her message with every stitch. The etiolated torso was elegant, and the vast swishing skirts enhanced her stately movements, but placed together they created an unfortunate foreshortening effect. Yet, such was her influence, her ladies-in-waiting and the ladies of the court followed the unflattering trend, and English skirts were worn slightly squared and shorter than those abroad.

Elizabeth loved to surround herself with beauty and, particularly fond of the combination of white with gold and silver, supplied her maids of honour with white gowns to

Lucy Harington, Countess of Bedford (Isaac Oliver, c. 1605). Pre-embroidered bodices were available from the Royal Exchange and popular among young ladies of the court. Queen Elizabeth I wears a similar garment in the Rainbow Portrait.

The Rainbow Portrait (attr. Marcus Gheeraerts, *c.* 1600). The snake symbolises the Queen's wisdom while the rainbow represents the peace and prosperity her reign has brought.

be worn at the most formal court occasions. Their virginal presence, like a flurry of angels escorting her, only served to glorify Gloriana. The key features were the open fan-shaped ruffs which were usually reserved for young unmarried women; false hanging sleeves so long that they fell behind the real sleeves past the vast drum-shaped farthingale, down to floor level; and a distinctive headdress of silver wire, pearls and spangles shaped to look like a cluster of delicate ferns and flowers. If in *Love's Labour's Lost* Shakespeare imagined the ladies-in-waiting to be dressed like Elizabeth's, the ruse of the princess having her ladies exchange their

The Pelican Portrait (Nicholas Hilliard, c. 1574), named after the pelican emblem on the jewel which dominates the Queen's bodice.

lovers' tokens and then appear masked to fool them is not so preposterous, as such an unnatural silhouette would have created an impression of uniformity that, unless they were significantly different in height, it would have been very difficult to tell them apart.

In the 1590s one of Elizabeth's young ladies-in-waiting, Lady Mary Howard made the foolish mistake of attempting to rival the Queen for the attention of the Earl of Essex. She bought herself a dress flounced with gold lace and pearls on sumptuous velvet, so beautiful it even impressed the jaded tastes of the court. Elizabeth was enraged – and in a

possibly rather apocryphal tale – took the dress while Mary was absent, and later appeared wearing it. When Elizabeth asked her if it was becoming, Mary sulkily replied that it was too short and the Queen retorted, 'If it become not me as being too short, I am minded it shall never become you as being too fine, so it fitteth neither well.'

Most people, however, took care to dress to please the Queen. Courtiers vied to be the most beautifully dressed in order to attract her attention, most famously Sir Walter Raleigh, who made a memorable first impression when he cast his expensively gorgeous cloak on the ground before her to cover a puddle.

Opposite: Detail from *Eliza Triumphans, Queen Elizabeth Being Carried in Procession* (attr. Robert Peake, c. 1601). Anne Russell, one of the Queen's favoured ladies in elegant court dress on her wedding day in Blackfriars, 1600 (see also picture on page 62).

Ball at the Court of Henri III (French School, c. 1581). Marguerite de Vaudemont demonstrates the advantage of the softer French farthingale and longer skirt length which allowed dresses to create their own sensual movement.

INDECENT BOSOMS AND BUM ROLLS

I N LINE WITH Elizabeth's tastes, the earlier part of the era was typified by a rigid double triangle silhouette of a large cone-shape Spanish farthingale, reflected by a small inverted triangle of bodice. Balance was achieved by heavy hanging sleeves, and contrast in a predominantly dark colour scheme by a beautifully embroidered pale partlet, placed beneath the bodice to define the slightly arched square bustline. Around 1585 a new silhouette began to appear, with a huge ruff balanced by wide trunk sleeves surrounding a slender bodice atop a large bell-shaped skirt. However, it was the vast drum farthingale that defined the later Elizabethan age.

With the change in silhouette came a complete change in values regarding modesty. Before the 1580s necklines were always high, concealing bound bosoms walled up behind stiff buckram bodies. But gradually the neckline opened up as the secret peek of smock became a decorative partlet, then the warm welcome of an open fan ruff, and finally an indecent scoop of décolletage that Nash describes in 1593: 'Their breasts they embusk up on high, and their round roseate buds immodestly lay forth to show at their hands there is fruit to be hoped.'

It was lamented that 'a ship is sooner rigged than a gentlewoman made ready' in Tomkis's 1602 play *Lingua,* which no doubt raised more than a few guffaws of recognition with the men of the audience, if not the ladies' maids! It is clear to see why from Peter Erondell's

Opposite;
Portrait of Anne Vavasour (John de Critz the Elder, c. 1605). A favoured maid of honour to Queen Elizabeth, she wears a splendid wheel farthingale decorated with ribbon rosettes.

Right: This ensemble shows the balanced silhouette of the 1570s, with gold chains pinned to the lady's bodice and partlet, and a matching chain girdle with pomander or 'dyle' (watch).

Far right: The transition between the cone and the drum farthingale was made in the 1580s via the bell-shape silhouette, which often placed a bum roll over a cone farthingale to soften the shape and widen the hips.

This lady of the court drawn by Nicholas Hilliard, c. 1585, is wearing the Spanish cone farthingale at its maximum 360-degree sweep with an embroidered fore-part secured by a series of bows.

The Infanta Isabella Clara Eugenia (Felippe de Liano, c. 1580). The fully closed high-necked bodice remained in fashion during the 1580s, especially in Spain.

The French Garden from 1586, in which the disagreeable Lady Rimellaine dresses to go out for a walk. First her maid warms her smock. After slipping into this the bodice of her petticoat is laced into place. Next she puts on her petticoat skirt, stockings and garters and, as she is to walk outside, her Spanish leather shoes. A carcenet is arranged around her throat – this was a heavy collar necklace of gold and jewels – and agate bracelets are added. The tailor is then ordered to bring in her open gown and farthingale. The neckwear – rebato or ruff – is chosen and pinned to

the bodice of the gown, and cuffs are added and pinned to sleeves. The farthingale and gown are added and the girdle is placed around the waist before she gathers her accessories: a mask, fan, comfit box, handkerchief, gloves and a rope of pearls.

The smock was the universal garment of underwear and sometimes worn in bed. It was changed and laundered frequently to keep the person fresh even if the stiff formal outer clothes were not laundry-friendly. It was often

Elizabeth of Austria, later Queen of France (after Francois Clouet, c. 1571), wears a full partlet to create a pleasing contrast to her bodice and to complement the puff in her sleeves.

In this portrait from 1569 the lady's ruff is embroidered in gold and her partlet, embroidered with red roses, is left slightly open to complement her stylish split-front bodice.

Portrait of Jacqueline Van Caestre (Peter Paul Rubens, c. 1617). Necklines opened up to allow for the fan ruff, which was particularly worn by young unmarried ladies as well as Queen Elizabeth I.

beautifully decorated with embroidery and lace at the neckline and cuffs so they could be displayed if a partlet was not worn.

The construction of the main kind of women's ensemble was a bodice or 'pair of bodies' with a separate skirt known as a kirtle or petticoat. The bodice was rigid and strengthened with busks of wood or whalebone that were slipped into channels stitched into the lining and tied into place with 'busk points' to stop them working their way out and digging into the wearer. The main busk centre front was often a piece of wood ornately carved as a love token from a beau to be worn close to her heart, for which she might give him a busk lace to wear as a favour in his hat.

The sleeves were separate, the points to tie them concealed by decorative 'wings' that could vary considerably in size and ornament. Often in the same fabric as the partlet – in contrast to the gown – they were beautifully decorative, frequently given as gifts or bestowed upon lovers as favours. A close-fitting sleeve, slightly padded and decorated with puffs and slashes was most usual, finished at the wrist with a hand ruff, but there was also a 'bishop' sleeve that was full from shoulder to wrist, ending in a tight cuff and hand ruff. Oversleeves were often worn, especially with the wheel farthingale, to balance out the width to the upper body, and, when extra long to reach the hem of the skirt, they created an elegant sweep to the aft.

From the Spanish word *verdugado* or the French *vertugale*, the farthingale was a petticoat of serviceable linen stitched with a series of channels set horizontally at intervals down the length of the skirt into which were inserted a series of hoops of cane, whalebone, steel or rush which increased in size as they neared the floor to create the signature cone shape. To conceal the ribs, this was then covered by an ordinary petticoat before the underdress – and sometimes overskirt – was arranged over the conical structure. At the opening of the sixteenth century the version first introduced by Katherine of Aragon was quite slender and demure, but as the decades passed it became wider and wider, becoming the foundation for a full 360° skirt, as worn by Elizabeth mostly in the late 1550s to early 1560s.

There had been various, mostly Puritan, denouncements against the Spanish farthingale suggesting that such a sinful papist fashion would deform the body, or allow concealment for the fruits of carnal knowledge, or, as Charles Barnsley fretted in *Shewing and Declaring the Pryde and Abuse of Women Now a Dayes*, that such 'bottell

Diagram of the Spanish farthingale showing the stiffened ribs.

arste bummes' would provide 'a bounsinge packsadel for the devyll to ryde on'. Hugh Latimer wrote in his *Remains and Sermons*, 'It is nothing but a token of fair pride to wear such vardingals.' But this was nothing in comparison to the suspicions levied against the drum farthingale which arrived from France in around 1586–8, as Stephen Gosson shows in his *Pleasant Quippes for Upstart Newfangled Gentlewomen*, 1596:

These hoopes that hippes and haunch do hide,
And heave aloft the gay hoist traine,
As they are now in use for pride,
So did they first begin in paine;
When whores in stewes had gotten poxe,
The French device kept coates from smocks.

The drum or wheel farthingale had the same principle of rods inserted into horizontal channels, but the rods were of equal size all the way down, creating a wide tube shaped like a drum. It was secured by a belt at the waist from which spokes set the cylinder of the skirt slightly off centre to be fairly flat below the stomacher, wide across the hips and with the greatest width to the back. Shakespeare suggests that widths were variable – in *The Two Gentlemen*

Detail from *The Sailing Wagon* (Claes Jansz. Visscher, c. 1606). The drum farthingale could be worn tilted, matching the angle sometimes used for cartwheel ruffs.

of Verona Julia enquires, 'What compass will you wear your farthingale?', while in *The Merry Wives of Windsor* Falstaff flatters Mistress Ford, telling her 'the firm fixture of thy foot would give an excellent motion to thy gait in a semi-circled farthingale'.

Several voluminous petticoats were required to soften the shape and ensure that the underdress draped in elegant folds so that the overdress would hang correctly from the shelf at hip level to ankle length. Some designs in the 1590s featured a valance of box pleating radiating out from the waist to the border of the hip-level plateau in imitation of the spokes of a wheel. The most fervent desire of one fourteen-year-old girl in Lancashire, 1597, was 'to have a French farthingale laid low before and high behind and broad on either side so I may laye mine arms on it'.

Known as an *hausse-cul* or 'bum roll' in England, and a *cache-enfant* in France, the French farthingale was padded bolster, tapered to a crescent shape like a croissant, tied around the waist above the under petticoats so the plump

The Farthingale and the Mask, c. 1600–10. A bum roll is tied into place, while another lady tries on a vizard mask, popularised by Venetian courtesans to give an air of mystery when attending the theatre.

part rested on the hips and bum at the back, and pulled in to create a neat roll along the point of the stomacher at the front. It had much the same effect as the wheel farthingale when worn with stiff brocades, but came into its own with the satins, silks and damasks of the French court, creating volume at the hips with sensuous movement that allowed the skirts to sweep inwards below the knee, kicking out at the hem. The softness of the skirt made it more practical for wearing when mounted on a horse, and for the more active lives of bourgeois women. It could also be worn over a Spanish cone-shape farthingale to pad the hips, making the skirt the fashionable bell shape of the 1580s.

The sixteenth-century corset made Victorian debutantes with their wasp waists look positively flabby! First spotted in 1533 in the trousseau of Catherine de Medici when she came to France as the thirteen-year-old bride of King Henry II, the cage corset was very effective, reducing her waist to a legendary 16 inches. Made of graduated strips of iron or pierced metal, it set the dimensions of the perfect slim torso and tiny waist, and once entrapped – by hinges one side and padlocks on the other – the body was forced to comply. There was a gap left to post the bosoms through, and each piece was bound with leather or velvet to provide some small comfort.

Mercifully the cage corset was little used after the 1580s as the new etiolated silhouette of the bodice highlighted by a decorative stomacher naturally drew the eye to emphasise the slenderness of the waist against the vast

A steel corset of pierced scrollwork from France, c. 1640. 'To become slender in the wast, … what pinching, will they not endure; yea sometimes with yron-plates, … [so] their very skin, and quicke flesh is consumed to the bones;' Montaigne's *Essays*, 1588.

Mary, Countess of Dorset (Marcus Gheeraerts the Younger, c. 1590s). Her stomacher is so long and narrow that it makes her torso appear the same width as her arm.

drum farthingale. Metalwork was still used to construct the front, with extremely long ribs trained to converge to a point as far below the waist as possible. The metal pieces were still bound in leather or velvet but were drawn in with tight lacing at the back instead. A less expensive and more practical alternative adopted by middle-class women was a basque or underbodice stiffened as before with pasteboard, busk and whalebone ribs but also conveniently laced at the back and without the improbable impeding length.

In *Pleasant Quippes for Upstart Newfangled Gentlewomen* Stephen Gosson describes corsets worn by men as well as women:

Those privie coats by art made strong,
With bones, with paste, and such like ware,
Whereby their backs and sides grow long.

There was a natural fertilisation of fashion between the courts of Europe as ambassadors came and went and gifts were exchanged. Even portraits provided inspiration, but deciphering the patterns could be very difficult. A more practical tool was the fashion doll which – first sent from the French court in 1396 – would arrive periodically, fully dressed in the latest fashions which could be interpreted by a skilled tailor to recreate the styles perfectly. Sometimes these 'French babies' would be made life-size so pattern cutting would be easier, but more often they were doll-size and usually passed to the daughters of the household to play with once their valuable message had been deciphered.

Fashions quickly filtered out from peripheral members of the court, but could take between five and fifteen years to reach those in the countryside. There might be opportunities to see the Queen and her glamorous ladies when she was on her progressions, to see the extravagant clothes of the travelling players, or to receive the latest fashion intelligence in letters from well-travelled friends, but without the chance to shop in London or any of the larger more prosperous cities, the materials available were seriously limited. Moderately sized

Lady Arabella Stuart (English School, 1577). The 23-month-old was the lucky recipient of a 'French baby' fashion doll, whose dress of the previous decade had rendered it obsolete as a fashion guide.

towns like Stratford-upon-Avon had a mercer, wool merchant, glover, tailor and hosier, but in many cases the best opportunity to shop would be the annual fair where girls like Overbury's romanticised milkmaid would happily spend their entire year's wages on the best fancy fripperies she could find. Her mistress, a wife of a yeoman farmer would be less spendthrift, but wouldn't miss the opportunity, both to wear her best when taking goods to market, and to shop.

There were second-hand clothes markets like that of London's Birchin Lane, but the risk of infection from plague from second-hand clothes no doubt fuelled a mistrust of someone wearing finer garments than one of their class could usually afford. There was also suspicion of itinerant pedlars, such as Autolycus from *The Winter's Tale*, but it didn't prevent excited villagers from gathering round to hear the latest ballad or news from London, or from pawing the beautiful 'ribands of all the colours i' the rainbow' which would be the best they would see until the annual fair.

AN INSOUCIANT CLOAK
AND A SHAPELY THIGH

MEN RESPONDED TO a woman in power by ditching their Henry VIII macho square silhouette in order to go for something far shapelier and more aesthetically pleasing in a feminisation of male styles. Men went to extreme lengths to present themselves to their best advantage and to represent their status, wealth and learning, even if they could be accused of telling a sartorial lie. There was an eclectic approach to fashion with a childlike joy in colour, pattern and decoration that would be considered overly ostentatious to the modern eye, and a grab-bag approach to international styles that presented a sartorial conundrum, as Portia highlights in her criticism of Falconbridge in *The Merchant of Venice*: 'How oddly he is suited! I think he bought his doublet in Italy, his round hose in France, his bonnet in Germany, and his behaviour everywhere.'

The most important garment for Elizabethan men was the doublet, originally a French style which first arrived in England in the fourteenth century. It was essential that it fitted well to display firm manly shoulders tapering in the desirable 'inverted triangle' silhouette into a narrow waist, especially so, if you wanted to impress a lady love. In *Much Ado About Nothing* Benedick comments on the love-struck Claudio: '… and now will he lie ten nights awake, carving the fashion of a new doublet.'

The Elizabethan tailor could employ considerable artistry; by widening the 'wings' at the shoulders, padding the chest and adding a buckram privie coat underneath to

Opposite:
Portrait of Sir Walter Raleigh (Attr. 'H' 1588). His splendid sable-lined cloak is adorned in a stunning sunburst pattern in seed pearls, while his white silk doublet fastens with pearl buttons along the peasecod, his black velvet-paned trunk-hose and girdle are decorated with them, and he wears a pearl bracelet and huge pearl earring.

Portrait of Robert Dudley, 1st Earl of Leicester (unknown artist, c. 1575). The Queen's favourite was regarded as an arbiter of taste, and his fine bearing is emphasised by the inverted triangle of his lightly pinked and slashed doublet with matching narrow-paned trunk hose.

pull in the waist he could transform a man! Doublet sleeves were separate and often of contrasting colour or decoration so as to add interest and a certain manly width without compromising the structure of the torso. They were attached by points, which were ribbons or narrow cords with metal ends or aiglets that would keep the ends from fraying and make it easier to thread through the eyelets concealed by the wings.

The 'peasecod belly' used a padding of canvas, buckram and even willow stems to distend the front of the doublet to a softly rounded point – like that at the end of a peapod – creating an apex which pointed emphatically at the place where the codpiece used to protrude. Originally a Dutch fashion, it became popular in around 1575 and remarkably remained at the forefront of fashion for over twenty years. This was understandable for those of portly stature like Falstaff whose image remains synonymous with his 'great belly doublet', but it was also warmly embraced by handsome young gallants, probably in connection with the game of wooing of a peasecod and its ability to divine true love.

Trunks and trunk-hose or, as Shakespeare refers to them, French hose or round hose, describe the combination of short breeches with stockings that met high up on the leg. Trunk-hose varied hugely in style throughout the period, from the vast French slops of gally-hose or galligaskins that sagged to just a couple of inches above the knee to a saucy micro-mini bum roll at the hips that originated at French court of Henri III in the later 1580s. Owing to the brevity of the trunk part, these were probably 'long-stocked' where the stockings were sewn on to make one garment. This hybrid arrangement first appeared around 1400 and remained current for the next two centuries, although after the mid-sixteenth century the term 'hose' began to refer exclusively to the upper breeches part, and especially after 1570 when separate stockings began to be worn.

Aside from extreme truncation, trunk-hose also had a period of extreme width, and they were so padded in the 1560s that they resembled large globular feminine buttocks – in the eyes of moralists at least! In 1562 there was an edict issued to tailors limiting the amount of material and stuffing they

A Young Man Leaning Against a Tree Among Roses (Nicholas Hilliard, c. 1588). He has no qualms showing off his legs, as in the poem 'Phyllida's Love-call, by wearing 'a pair of stockings white as milk' upon his 'legs so tall'.

Portrait of King Charles IX (François Clouet, c. 1566). His jerkin has long flared skirts to accommodate his huge globular or 'onion' trunk-hose.

could use to prevent 'the monstrous and outrageous greatness of hosen'. Any tailor found to be making them more capacious would be banned from practising his trade, and the transgressors who wore them would be prosecuted under the 'Acts of Apparel'. A contemporary account from the Harleian Manuscripts attests that a young man accused of stuffing his trunk-hose to excess was brought before the court:

He drew out of his breeches a pair of sheets, two table-cloaths, ten napkins, four shirts, a brush, a glasse, a combe, and night-caps, with other things of use, saying, your lordship may understand that because I have no safer storehouse, these pockets do serve for a roome to lay my goods in ...

The usual bombast was less inventive; frequently a strong inner lining of canvas or bayes (wool cloth) stuffed with hair, sometimes in a padded roll worn at the hips, or even two smaller rolls around the thighs.

The 'short blistered breeches' referred to in Shakespeare's *Henry VIII* were French hose artistically slashed to allow the soft lining material to be pulled through in puffs. Giving a rich and vivid contrast in colour and texture, they provided numerous edges to be dressed with lace, braid or embroidery. Slashing or paning was the most popular form of decoration – for menswear especially. There was something wanton in slashing the expensive velvet, silk, satin or damask of doublet and hose implying not only careless conspicuous consumption, but a cruel contempt for the rich luxurious fabrics that the lower classes would love to be able to afford – or be allowed to wear. Some slashed or paned hose were not quite as glamorous as they appeared;

closer examination revealed that the velvet panes carefully edged with braid were in fact small panels stitched carefully at top and bottom onto an existing garment.

Large and full, Venetian hose were described by Stubbes as breeches that 'reach beneath the knee to the gartering-place of the legge, where they are tied finely with silken points, or some such like, and laid on also with rows of lace or gardes'. References to this long hose appear in household accounts and wardrobe inventories of the playhouses, but although Shakespeare mentions 'venetian tire' in general, there is no mention of venetians. Early forms in the 1570s fitted snugly to the thigh and were worn with stockings pulled up over them and gartered above the knee, but they were most popular in their fullest or pear-shaped form during the 1580s–90s.

Everywhere was upholstered and remodelled except for the legs, which were regarded as one of men's finest features. According to Thomas Dekker in his play *The Honest Whore, Part 1* (1604) all the protagonist could wish for was a 'kind gentleman … indifferent handsome [but] meeyly limbed and thighed', while Juliet's nurse in *Romeo and Juliet* comments – somewhat inappropriately – that 'though

The Banner Bearer (Hendrick Goltzius, 1587). It has been suggested that slashing originated on the battlefield when soldiers stripped clothes from bodies and stuffed them inside their own for warmth. The resulting effect created heavy padding in certain areas with the foreign colours peeping through the tattered remnants of their own battle scarred uniforms.

Sir Martin Frobisher (Cornelius Ketel, 1577), is wearing voluminous venetians with a leather jerkin left slightly undone to reveal the points which fasten his breeches to the doublet.

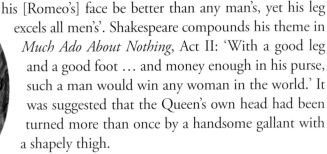

his [Romeo's] face be better than any man's, yet his leg excels all men's'. Shakespeare compounds his theme in *Much Ado About Nothing*, Act II: 'With a good leg and a good foot … and money enough in his purse, such a man would win any woman in the world.' It was suggested that the Queen's own head had been turned more than once by a handsome gallant with a shapely thigh.

Such shapeliness was enhanced by exquisitely expensive silk stockings imported from Italy that would be treasured and re-dyed if their shade went out of fashion. In *Twelfth Night* Malvolio wears yellow stockings which are cross-gartered 'most villainously; like a pedant that keeps a school i' the church'. Unfortunately, being one of Shakespeare's most conceited characters he is easily flattered and deceived by the forged letter which says 'remember who commended thy yellow stockings, and wished to see thee ever cross-gartered' and so he is fooled into appearing before his love Olivia in 'a colour she abhors' and 'a fashion she detests'.

Unknown Man Against a Background of Flames (attr. Nicholas Hilliard, c. 1590). His falling lace-edged collar is left open to display the miniature of his lady-love, while the flames symbolise his passion.

Sir Christopher Hatton (Cornelius Ketel, c. 1575). Canions were the tubular extensions that segued from the puff of the trunk-hose at upper thigh, down to the knee. This allowed separate stockings to be worn drawn up and gartered over them.

Cross-gartering was a pedantic method of tying the garters where each garter was placed straight below the knee, crossed behind, and the ends brought forward to be fastened with a flourish just above the patella. This would keep the stocking smooth both above and below the joint, with the aim of minimising bagging and wrinkling.

It fell out of fashion towards the end of the reign of James I, becoming the province of May dancers and Morris men. It was a sign of status to be able to go garter-free, firstly to show exquisitely expensive perfectly fitting stockings, but also to display legs so shapely they didn't require gartering. To keep garters properly tied could be a pest, and in *King Lear* the Fool puns 'he wears cruel garters. Horses are tied by the heads … men by the legs.'

It was bad form for a gentleman to appear in public without either a cloak or gown over his doublet. In *Romeo and Juliet* stage directions have Capulet making his entry 'in his gown' to denote the gravitas of his status. However, there was a general move away from the gown whose capacious folds and fur edges were so much a feature of Henry VIII's court; by the 1570s this sober costume was more the province of older gentlemen, academics and town grandees.

For the sake of comfort and warmth at home, a full length silk or satin fur-lined gown was often worn. Known as a nightgown, it fell in folds suspended from a yoke, with a deep falling collar that turned into revers down the front edges, and the same hanging sleeves as a regular gown. It was a more attractive warm layer to be put on when going down to breakfast, or as in the Scottish play, when frolicking around a castle at night trying to cover up a murder! Lady Macbeth hears knocking at the south entry after Duncan's murder; she tells her husband:

Get on your nightgown, lest occasion call us
And show us to be watchers.'

A German Courtier, c. 1580. As Shakespeare joked in *Much Ado about Nothing*, he is '… a German from the waist downward, all slops …'. He is also wearing his stockings cross-gartered like the unfortunate Malvolio.

Worn with the insouciant casual air of one of Elizabeth's favourite explorers, the cloak became the most glamorous and often most expensive item of male apparel. The Spanish cloak was short but full and had a hood, although often more for ornament than practicality; the Dutch cloak had wide sleeves which were left hanging loose, while the French cloak was the most dashing. Thrown nonchalantly over the left shoulder and fastened under the arm, it varied in length, reaching knee and even ankle length during the 1580s. It could be cut lavishly in a full circle, or 'full compass' or semicircular 'half compass' and it often also had a deep shoulder cape reaching to elbow length. The most ornate style of cloak, it was often decorated with bugle beads or pearls, or 'guarded' with bands of velvet or lace.

In *The Tempest* the 'glistering apparel' of Prospero's wardrobe on the boat included a jerkin and a gown that Caliban, Stephano and Trinculo dressed themselves in. Caliban also had a long voluminous cloak described as a gabardine. This was not an unusual garment for Venetians of professional rank, but Jewish people were forced to wear it with a yellow hood to denote the 'shame' of their race

La Première Partie du Compte de Richard Cooke, 1584. The serving men at the court of Henri III of France wear short French cloaks with hanging sleeves, decorative hoods, or 'guarded' with bands of contrasting fabric.

and religion. When Antonio comes to borrow money from Shylock in *The Merchant of Venice*, the moneylender is reluctant to fulfil his request, reminding him that not days before, he spat upon his 'Jewish gaberdine' with derision and called him a 'cut-throat dogge'.

The mandilion was pure Elizabethan eccentricity. Originally a military garment, it came into fashion around 1577, reaching the height of its popularity in the 1580s, before being relegated as an item for livery after 1620. A cross between a jacket and a cloak, it was hip-length and loose because the side seams were left open and the sleeves hanging. It had a small standing collar and was fastened from throat to chest to allow it to be put on over the head when it was then whipped round 90° 'Colley-Westonward' – a Cheshire term for something going awry – so that the front and back panels swept the shoulders and the sleeves hung deflated front and back.

The gorget was the perfect accessory to display military prowess, as it combined armour with civilian dress without destroying the effect of a fashionable ensemble. It was only permissible for military men to wear, but nevertheless there were more than a few who adopted a military swagger they weren't entitled to. John Marston in his poem 'The Scourge of Villainy' is unstinting in his scorn of the bombasted hero who claims to have seen active service and peppers his language with 'cannon-oaths' and adopts martial poses as if to prove it, but he is just a clothes horse: 'naught but clothes and scenting sweet perfume', 'drawn and quartered with lace' and not really a man but 'an incarnate devil That struts in vice and glorieth in evil'.

Yet there was also suspicion and even fear of those who were too effeminate. In *The Merry Wives of Windsor* Falstaff refers to dandies as 'lisping hawthorn-buds, that come like women in men's apparel, and smell like Bucklersbury [an area of London renowned for apothecaries and perfumers using exotic spices]

Robert Sidney, 1st Earl of Leicester (unknown artist, 1588). The subject cuts a dashing figure with his mandilion worn 'Colley-Westonward' with a scarf as ensign of his military rank.

in simple time'. In the Bible Moses makes it clear (Deuteronomy 22:5) that wearing the garments of the opposite gender was an 'abomination unto the Lord thy God' and would ultimately lead to sexual confusion and the breakdown of society. No wonder, then, that some of the moralists were terrified by the wrongs perpetrated in the theatre, assuming – sometimes correctly – that the young men made beautiful in women's apparel would be a source of lustful fascination to the more experimental or less discerning of the audience.

Sir Philip Sidney (unknown artist c. 1576). As befits a man of military honour, he wears a gorget edged with gold engraving, complemented by the gold braid decorating his black velvet paned trunk-hose and codpiece.

The codpiece was in shrinking decline by Shakespeare's time, but in *The Two Gentlemen of Verona*, whilst she is helping Julia disguise herself as a man, Lucetta refers to it as a handy device for storing pins. Possibly as part of the feminisation of fashion, the codpiece became far less tumescent after 1570; nestling within the folds of the trunk-hose, it was still a safe place to keep a purse and handkerchief, and even oranges to be handed out to the ladies, possibly as a treat at the theatre. It finally went out of use in the 1590s, presumably once the fruit bowl was discovered!

RUFFS AND REBATOS

As ELIZABETHAN FASHION was notoriously changeable and eclectic, the best way to keep abreast was to update accessories and change trimmings. Those who couldn't make it to the Royal Exchange could find a selection of pretty novelties in more prosperous cities at milliners' shops – named after Milan where many of their finest fripperies came from – but haberdashers would also be worth a look, and for the leaner pocket, itinerant pedlars, such as Autolycus in *The Winter's Tale*, could carry some unexpected treasures:

> Lawn as white as driven snow, Cyprus black as ere a crow,
> Gloves as sweet as damask roses, masks for faces and for noses,
> Bugle bracelet, neckless-amber, perfume for my lady's chamber,
> Golden coifs and stomachers for my lads to give their dears,
> Pins and poking sticks of steel, what maids lack from head to heel ...

The ruff was the signature of the Elizabethan era. It started life as a humble decorative edge to the smock and grew in every possible way, stiffening to ensnare the face, presenting the head on a platter like that of John the Baptist dressed with a doily. During the 1560s it became a separate band that could be decorated and dressed in ever more extravagant ways.

Opposite: *Portrait of Mary Fitton* (attr. Gower, c. 1600). The mysterious Mary Fitton was suddenly excused from her duties as lady in waiting to Elizabeth, c. 1600, when her daring dalliance with Lord Pembroke produced an illegitimate child, provoking a scandal that led to her banishment and his imprisonment. Her vast hanging sleeves have striking serrated edges with wired sprigs of pearls.

The outer edge was decorated with embroidery, cutwork or lace, while the inner edge was threaded with a string that, when drawn tight, created both the folds of the ruff and the method of fastening it at the front. A cord could also be stitched at the outer edge, adding a certain stiffness, and a charming wibbly effect, but the arrival of starch from Holland in 1560 was a revolution. The stylish regarded it as something akin to alchemy – making soft folds stiff, and, of course, for the same reason, the Puritans condemned it as the devil's liquor. Even with such an innovation, to set a ruff properly was very labour-intensive, as each flute of the ruff was set individually with a poking stick. Made of wood or bone, this was pushed into each fold and carefully smoothed to create a 'set' of perfect even loops in a figure-of-eight formation.

In 1573 steel poking sticks became available. These were more efficient and gave a better effect, allowing ruff size to increase, and the time saved could be dedicated to setting matching hand ruffs. Because the steel poking sticks could be heated directly in the fire, it allowed the starch-pasted ruff to be not just dried into place but practically crisped into rigidity. Once set to perfection the ruff was

Aping of Fashion, caricature, *c.* 1580. In the middle of the foreground one ape is heating the poking sticks in a brazier while another is creating the sets on a special ruff stand, and in the background yet others hang the completed ruffs to ensure they dry perfectly before being sent to their intended recipients.

packed carefully in a band box – like a shallow hat box – for delivery to its owner. Ruffs were sometimes carried like this when a lady was attending a party so there was no chance it could become dishevelled during her journey, and she would have it pinned on when she arrived.

Philip Stubbes complains in 1583 of the ruff's ever-increasing size: 'they have great and monsterous ruffs, made either of cambric, holland, lawn, whereof some be a quarter of a yard deep'. The ruff known as the 'three steps and a half to the gallows' was a three-piled ruff; according to Thomas Dekker and Thomas Middleton's play *The Honest Whore, Part 1* (1604) 'the fashion, three falling one upon another (for that's the new edition now)'.

Mrs Holland (lady-in-waiting to Elizabeth I), aged twenty-six (Nicholas Hilliard, 1593). She wears an impressive three-piled ruff edged with sprigs of pearls, which Stubbes condemned as 'a more monstrous kind of ruff'.

Various tints of vegetable dye could be applied at the starch stage to produce pink, mauve or yellow shades more flattering to many complexions than the standard slightly ivory white of the linen or lawn used. Smalt, a mixture of cobalt and ground glass, was used rather than woad or indigo to give a lasting blue, but in 1591 R. Greene commented in *A Notable Discovery of Cosenage* that blue starch was favoured by prostitutes, describing 'these streetwalkers … in ruffs of the largest size … gloried richly with blue starch'. This might have prompted the Queen's decree of 1595 to ban blue ruffs, suggesting that instead cochineal should be added to make them mauve. However, in Thomas Platter's *Travels in England* (1599) the author found that 'the womenfolk of England who have mostly blue grey eyes, and are fair and pretty … lay great store by ruffs and starch them blue so that their complexion shall appear whiter'.

Saffron starch was also very fashionable before the stench of scandal destroyed its gilded lustre. In 1613 Countess

Frances Howard was aided and abetted in the poisoning of
Sir Thomas Overbury by Anne Turner, a court dressmaker
who worked with Inigo Jones presumably in the creation of
his masque designs. She was holder of the patent for saffron

starch, but this devil's liquor was not the only sorcery she was a party to, and it was revealed at her trial in 1616 that she had used French fashion dolls to represent the people who were the subject of her spells. Frances had confessed before the trial and was eventually pardoned, but against such serious charges Anne had no reprieve.

Her executioner wore the saffron ruff and cuffs that she made fashionable, giving an unnecessarily cruel and mocking note to the proceedings, and so giving an ignominious ending to the fashion. Moral commentators were quick to blame the vanity and folly of women enjoying such fashions as the root cause of such a dreadful scandalous affair and saffron starch was axed as efficiently as Anne was. Shakespeare makes fun of Parolles in *All's Well That Ends Well* as 'a snipt-taffeta fellow', his great ruff starched with 'villanous saffron'.

When worn with a doublet, the high neckline would keep a small ruff pert around the jawline, but for larger ruffs a supportasse was required, especially to give the jaunty 'tipped up at the back, down in front' look that was so popular in the 1610s. This construction of wire 'whipped over either with gold, thread, silver or silk' was pinned to the doublet so the ruff could be pinned to it – a process that could take hours. There was also the pickadil, another type of supportasse with tabs laid out horizontally to support the ruff or standing collar. A Mr Higgins, a London tailor based in St James's *c.* 1600–20 set up an establishment to cope with the demand, calling his supportasses 'picadillies' and so gave the name to the famous area in London.

The open, fan-shape ruff was usually worn by unmarried women, and for more ceremonial occasions it remained

Opposite: *Queen Anne of Denmark (Paul Van Somer, 1617).* Wife of James I, Queen Anne enjoyed the brief vogue for saffron starch with her bold whisk collar and pretty, matching golden lace.

The 'True Portrait' of Lady Frances Howard (Simon van de Passe, *c.* 1618–20), an engraving from the portrait by William Larkin, *c.* 1615. Her large pristine ruff is in striking contrast to her daring décolleté.

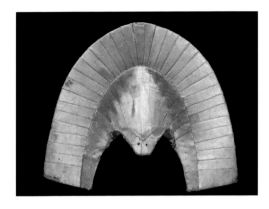

popular with the extremely décolleté gowns worn at the Jacobean court. The rebato was fashionable from 1580 to 1635, and seemingly began as the term for a collar very similar to the fan ruff, but after 1600 the term was transferred to the support. Usually made of wire and trimmed with a

Picadil supportasse, 1610–15. Carefully constructed in stiff pasteboard, this has been shaped to fit the shoulders of the wearer and covered with strips of ivory silk to conform to the curved shape.

A Spanish Lady (Alonso Sanchez-Coello, *c.* 1600). Spanish ladies were known for their ornate ruffs and rebatos. This superb concoction of bone lace is supported by a rebato of gilded wire edged by teardrop pearls.

pointy lace-like reticella, the rebato was very ornate and could be worn in several layers, commanding much time and effort as Nashe bemoaned in his 1593 *Christ's Tears Over Jerusalem*: 'I see Gentlewomen ... burning out many pounds of candle in pinning their treble rebaters.'

Images of Shakespeare show him in a standing band type of collar sometimes known as a 'whisk' – or, in Spain, a 'golilla' – which became a fashion choice at the turn of the century. This is sometimes taken to mean that he didn't care for the ruff which he rarely mentions except to criticise in *All's Well That Ends Well* but for Shakespeare it might have seemed more forward-thinking to have a portrait depicting himself in a newer fashion. Maybe he just preferred the smooth lines that the whisk offered, with an emphatic horizontal underlining the face, and a pristine semicircle of lawn framing the head behind. Although Shakespeare's is very plain, the definite lines of this kind of collar are almost always highlighted by a rich edging of cutwork or Vandyked lace.

One of the most striking features of many of Queen Elizabeth's outfits were the gauzy butterfly wings that delicately framed her as the Faerie Queen of Spenser's poetic tribute. This veil was a very large square of gauze edged all round in lace, cutwork or reticella. It was elaborately placed to stunning effect with the point of one corner placed at the hairline or attached to the headdress, gathered over the head into the nape of the neck, from where it was wired out in wings to each side of the head, coming forward over the shoulders, it

The Cobbe Portrait of Shakespeare, commissioned from an unknown artist by Shakespeare's patron Sir Henry Wriothesley, c. 1610. It depicts Shakespeare looking unusually young and stylish in a beautiful 'whisk' collar edged with valuable lace.

slipped behind and acted as a frame for the large ruff. The wire was secured to the bodice at the side of the bosom in front of the armpit from where the loose volume of the veil fell over the sleeves and down the back allowing the fourth corner to trail behind the skirts.

Elizabeth's delight in wearing her hair uncovered gave everyone else permission to do so, and as her reign advanced so did the art of hairdressing, as hair was whisked high off the forehead and dressed with jewels. Until 1600 hats were usually only worn for riding, travelling and in the country. Fashionable hats were distinctly masculine,

Court Lady Once Thought to be Queen Elizabeth I (attr. Lucas de Heere, c. 1590s). The wired 'fairy wings' edged in pearls have an added border of large standing pearls.

such as a stylised top hat with ostrich plume and jewels. More matronly ladies and those in the country maintained a more substantial headdress that was usually also worn under the hat, whereas more fashionable ladies wore a reticulated caul underneath offering a prettier contrast.

Ophelia was amazed to see Hamlet appear 'with no hat upon his head', as men wore hats most of the time, including while dining, and at home. They also utilised them in various ways: as part of certain dances, to parry thrusts while fighting, or to raise it with a flirtatious flourish to greet a pretty lady; whichever way, it would be replaced immediately. No handsome young gallant could resist pointing out their allure by wearing a favour from a lover in their hatband like the daring knights of old. Handkerchiefs, gloves and ribbons all made good favours; a line from *Hamlet* asserts 'a very riband in the cap of youth'.

Beautifully made of the finest leathers, richly embroidered with coloured silks, gold lace, tassels and silk ribbon gussets with fashionably long fingers to emulate the elegant royal hands, gloves were emblematic of status. To display the wearer's extreme leisure, they looked striking when in repose but rather idiotically crumpled in use. A popular wedding favour, gloves epitomised romance and were often given as love tokens showing the giver would forever serve the recipient, but throwing down the gauntlet was an incontrovertible challenge that no gentleman could refuse.

Another romantic gesture was to embroider a handkerchief as a love token for a beau by 'printing one's thoughts in lawn'; however, sometimes such love tokens could be tragically misused as in *Othello*. The Moor gives his wife Desdemona a handkerchief embroidered with strawberries, an innocent token of love until it falls into the

Unknown Man Clasping Hand from a Cloud (Nicholas Hilliard, 1588). His elegant hat with high 'bowler'-style crown and jewelled band are the height of fashion, as is his falling band of reticella lace.

perfidious hands of Emilia whose 'wayward husband hath a hundred times Woo'd me to steal it'. Iago then has evidence to back up his claim of Desdemona's unfaithfulness with Cassio when he insists 'such a handkerchief – I am sure it was your wife's – did I today See Cassio wipe his beard with.' Othello inevitably reacts to the 'poison poured in his ear', and the tragedy is set.

Usually worn when the waistline was at its natural level in the 1560–70s, the girdle provided attractive emphasis to the waistline of gown or doublet, suspending a jewelled

Gloves presented to Queen Elizabeth I on her visit to Oxford University in 1566. Du Maurier wrote that, during an audience with various ambassadors, she pulled off her gloves more than a hundred times to display her beautiful, white hands.

pomander, muff, or even a watch known as a 'dyle' for women; men's almost always supported a sheath for a sword or dagger and often both. A demiceint was a less expensive version where the back portion of the chain was substituted with plain silk. The fan could also be worn suspended from the girdle. Usually circular, they were often made of swans' down and ostrich plumes and sometimes concealed a valuable mirror in the centre. Especially useful to add a fluttering accent to a flirtatious gaze, the folding fan appeared around 1580 and was regarded as quite a status symbol. Other fans were embroidered silk or velvet like little flags – the long elegant handles were bejewelled gold, silver or agate and, beautiful enough to make an impressive gift, they were also a prime target for thieves, as Falstaff insinuates to Pistol in *The Merry Wives of Windsor*. It was usually an article entrusted to a lady-in-waiting who would follow, wafting her mistress gently, or, as in *Love's Labour's Lost*, to an admirer such as Don Armado: 'a most dainty man! To see him walk before a lady and to bear her fan!'

When the Spanish ambassador Gondomar was at the court of King James I in 1600 he told the King, 'I shall amaze my countrymen by letting them know at my return that all London is booted and apparently ready to walk out of town.' Beautiful boots were particular to England, expensive and luxurious; the over-the-knee boots were

Flea Fur Belonging to the Duchess of Bavaria (Hans Mülich, c. 1550). One flea fur given to Queen Elizabeth I had a gold head and feet and was 'garnished with dyamonds and rubyes'.

Portrait of a Young Man (Isaac Oliver, 1590–5). Boot hose were sturdy overstockings worn with boots to protect the costly stockings, but even these practical garments could be ornate.

Opposite: *Richard Sackville Earl of Dorset* (Isaac Oliver, 1615). Silk stockings like these in blue with gold-embroidered clocks were the height of fashion, as were the white leather shoes topped by huge rosettes '*big enough to hide a cloven foot,*' as Ben Jonson wrote in The *Devil is an Ass.*

made of leather or russet cloth sometimes with elaborate embroidered tops, fringes or turnovers. Boots or buskins were universal for riding, and, after 1585, for walking. Military men looked especially dashing in their thigh boots turned over to reveal lace-topped boot hose, and men with unattractive skinny legs like Thurio in *The Two Gentlemen of Verona* were quick to realise that they could disguise them with attractive well-cut boots.

Wearing pretty shoes in the ordure of the streets was out of the question and most country women wore pattens as a kind of overshoe, consisting of a foot-shaped wooden platform balanced on a ring of iron that would keep shoes and skirts out of muck and mud. From Venice, chopines were a far loftier version made of cork or wood and covered in velvet, which raised the wearer in height by 18 inches or more, and almost as much in status. Worn in Venice from the fifteenth century, chopines were adopted in England c. 1590–1610. As Hamlet noted, 'Your ladyship is nearer heaven than when I last saw you by the altitude of a chopine'; but, as Ben Jonson ridiculed, 'they tread on corked stilts at a pris'nors pace'. Chopines were notoriously difficult to walk in, yet those who managed it were thought to sashay in the most sensual way, although they were possibly somewhat encumbered by the dwarves reputedly required to attend their every pace, to allow them to rest their elbows upon their heads!

Although moral opinion was against cosmetics, under Elizabeth's influence they were increasingly used to whiten

Venetian chopines c. 1600, made of carved pine covered with white kid leather in a punched design. Heights of 30 inches were not uncommon in Venice, though the highest known in England; this pair was more practical at 7.5 inches high.

Robert Devereux, 2nd Earl of Essex (attr. Marcus Gheeraerts, c. 1596). His square-cut beard is dyed a startling red in emulation of the Queen's auburn hair.

complexions and add roses to maidenly cheeks, albeit with artificial lead based 'peints'. Elizabethans were groomed and perfumed to complement their rich apparel wearing a tint of alkanet lip rouge, patches, masks and jewels in their hair. By 1613 London was regarded as a 'school of vanity' with most ladies wearing some kind of make-up if only to appear at their most gorgeous when visiting the Exchange, the theatre or King James's court, where even his lords had taken on the appearance of 'a brace of painted creatures'.

PAGEANTRY, MASQUE AND THEATRE

THE WIDESPREAD INTEREST in fashion during Shakespeare's era went hand in hand with the proliferation of performance, as the burgeoning modern economy stimulated a nascent interest in self-expression, and through the Bard's witty quill and the enduring love of his works the two have remained inextricably linked. There had always been a love of the magical transformation of costume and performance from the days of pagan ritual, through the medieval and Tudor religious plays, but the Elizabethans transferred their use from sober spiritual reflection to the mischievous fun of the Lord of Misrule.

Gloriana co-opted the power of costume and pageantry as one of her greatest PR tools lending gravitas to her every move. Her annual progressions blessed her people with the opportunity to worship in the wake of a dazzling procession featuring the Queen and her lords and ladies, cutting a dash with an entourage of servants and over 600 cartloads of essential possessions. It also gave her the opportunity to exhibit her love of her people, learning benevolently of their needs and sharing in their successes as detailed in Nichol's *Progresses of the Queen*; when she visited Norwich in 1578 the 'Pageant of the Artizan Strangers' was given to demonstrate for her their artistry in worsted textiles.

Entertainment was hugely important to the court and every occasion was celebrated with some extravagant display. Crownation Day on 17 November celebrated Elizabeth's accession to the throne. Each year it was marked

Opposite detail from *Eliza Triumphans, Queen Elizabeth being carried in Procession* (attr. Robert Peake, c. 1601). As Paulus Hentzer observed in 1598: 'Wherever she turned her face as she was going along, everybody fell down on their knees. The ladies of the court followed next to her, very handsome and well shaped, and for the most part dressed in white.' (See also picture on page 26.)

Queen Elizabeth Dancing with the Earl of Leicester (unknown artist, c. 1580s). La Volta was an energetic form of the Galliard where, holding the lady around the waist, the man grabbed her intimately at the base of her busk to propel her into the air!

by a lavish tournament staged by her finest knights in their most glamorous armour as they vied to win her attention by presenting the most fabulous gift. However, the Earl of Leicester trumped any gift or entertainment ever offered to the Queen, when during her stay at Kenilworth Castle in 1575, in his determination to finally win her hand, he created a stunning pageant with masked *commedia dell'arte* players, the centrepiece casting Gloriana as King Arthur and himself as her most worthy champion.

George Clifford 3rd Earl of Cumberland (Nicholas Hilliard, c. 1590). The Queen's Champion at the Tilt looks dashing in his tournament costume with the Queen's glove as a favour in his hat, but he has thrown down the challenging gauntlet.

From the days of Henry VIII there had been a dedicated Revels Office run as part of the royal household where commissions were made, scenery and costumes designed and procured, and theatrical players auditioned. There was a handsome budget, and a fortune was spent on costumes of the highest quality to ensure that they dazzled in the intimate setting of the court. Although the accounts at the Revels Office show that many costumes were recycled, often the company commissioned would be able to keep them as part of their payment – kudos that would be of massive value as they travelled elsewhere.

This tradition was echoed by the nobility, who frequently opened their great halls to entertainers. When visiting England, the sixteenth-century diarist and schoolmaster Thomas Platter of Basle wrote:

> The players wear the most costly and beautiful dresses, for it is the custom in England that when noblemen or knights die, they leave their finest clothes to their servants, who, since it would not be fitting for them to wear such splendid garments, sell them soon afterwards to the players for a small sum.

Lady in Masque Costume, miniature by Isaac Oliver. The lady is dressed in the style of Inigo Jones' costumes for Ben Jonson's masques performed at the court of James I.

The masque became hugely popular at court and beyond; it was an interesting way to alleviate the boredom and ennui of a purely decorative life and to express oneself while showcasing a talent for poetry, dance or tournament skills. Most of all, it was a wonderful opportunity to attract favour and enchant potential suitors. After Anne Boleyn's success with advertising her charms at court masques, the opportunity for graceful display could not be missed – especially if dressed in a diaphanous chemise like the costume for a nymph designed by Bernardo Buontalenti in 1589: '… that though the length of it reached her ankles, yet in her going one might sometimes discern the small of her leg'.

Masque costume design for a Fiery Spirit for Thomas Campion's *Lord's Maske*, 1613 by Inigo Jones.

Mary Sidney, Countess of Pembroke (Paul Van Somer, c. 1610). The mantle draped from the left shoulder and the narrower bell-shaped skirt is redolent of the *Costume for Tethys*, and similar to many of the early seventeenth-century portraits of court ladies wearing masque costume.

The risqué costumes caused more than a little excitement and helped to maintain the popularity of the masque, especially in the Jacobean court when it became de rigueur for beautiful young courtiers to have their portraits painted in masque costume as Grecian goddesses or wood nymphs, picturesquely semi-draped, revealing alabaster shoulders and even a perfect breast which was thought to suggest maiden purity with the promise of lush fruitfulness. This may well have contributed to the steep descent of the décolletage during the early 1600s into unabashed nudity when young unmarried women wore bodices scooped so low that their breasts were completely exposed.

Queen Anne's pride in her perfect smooth pale bosom led her always to wear extremely low-cut bodices. In 1617 the Venetian ambassador in his dispatches described Queen Anne as wearing a bodice that displayed her bosom 'bare down to the pit of the stomach', adding that English women dress 'so well and lasciviously as to defy exaggeration' and asserting 'the plump and buxom display their bosoms very liberally'. He also commented on her farthingale, 'four feet wide', which Anne had insisted remain part of formal court wear despite King James's various attempts to ban it, especially in 1616 after an unfortunate incident when a group of revellers became wedged in the entrance to the masquing hall, causing an accident. Unrepentant, Anne kept her farthingale, and it was only retired from court attire after her death in 1619.

Another pleasure of masque costume was the vizard mask sometimes worn, the concealment of identity providing a frisson of romantic mystery even with so much flesh revealed. Ladies of the court who wished to sample the delights of the public theatres incognito would attend even the most ribald plays wearing their vizards to protect their anonymity while also claiming all eyes, creating sufficient stir to seize the audience's attention until the actors took to the stage.

Costume for Tethys [Goddess of the Ocean] in 'Tethys Festival' (Samuel Daniel, 1610). During the Jacobean reign the exposure of a lady's breasts was commonplace and the shorter narrower bell-shape farthingale influenced wider fashion.

Early XVIIth Century Lowlanders (unknown artist). In 1616 a treatise by Thomas Tuke denounced women not only for displaying their breasts, but for whitening them with ceruse and even rouging their nipples with cochineal.

Orazio Busino, chaplain to the Venetian ambassador to the court of James I, described his visit to the Fortune Theatre in 1617 or 1618: 'These theatres are frequented by a number of respectable and handsome ladies, who come freely and seat themselves amongst the men without the slightest hesitation.' He found himself somewhat uncomfortably in the midst of 'a bevy of young women' but managed to take in plenty of detail of the attire of one 'very elegant dame' who wore a mask; 'this lady's bodice was of yellow satin richly embroidered, her petticoat of gold tissue with stripes, her robe of red velvet with a raised pile, lined with yellow muslin with broad stripes of pure gold'.

The theatre also attracted the dandies of the Elizabethan era, the 'Gulls', so named by Thomas Dekker in '*The Gull's Hornbook*' – his facetious guide for those who wished to join the ranks of squawking popinjays who took the stools at the edge of the stage to show off their ostentatious outfits rather than to enjoy the play. They would arrive late and noisy:

> Present not yourself on the stage, especially at a new play, until the prologue hath by rubbing got colour into his cheeks, and is ready to give the trumpets their cue that he's upon point to enter …

This dramatic entrance should, of course, be followed up by laughing loudly during the most serious part of the tragedy, and talking loudly throughout the rest, criticising the acting and costumes – anything to annoy actors and audience alike!

In *Christ's Tears Over Jerusalem* the Puritan Thomas Nashe criticised theatre in general, adding that the 'overlashing in apparel is so common a fault'. Wearing beautiful clothes was regarded as being almost synonymous with being an actor, and in some cases, sufficient for admittance into the dubious profession. In *Hamlet* the Prince of Denmark asks Horatio whether 'a forest of feathers … with two Provincial roses on my razed shoes' would earn him 'a fellowship in a cry of players'? Such glamour was one of the many reasons why the Puritans condemned actors as purveyors of deception who were rabble-rousers and seduced impressionable maidens before travelling on.

The allure was powerful and universal. Just as the English Renaissance brought forth a flowering of self-expression in poetry and art, theatre – unlike art and poetry which remained largely inaccessible to the majority – could be experienced at different levels in society. Although there would be almost no similarity between the life of a lady of the court and that of a capper from Coventry, they would both be able to enjoy the works of Shakespeare, and quite possibly see them performed by the same actors in the same costumes, even if one saw the plays as they were premiered before the Queen and the other saw them performed in the local guildhall. They would also be able to enjoy them in the same ways, for the pleasure of entertainment, and for the delight of costumes that had originated in the creative inner sanctum of the court. Where the art engaged them, mirroring real human emotion, the costumes on the stage, the fashions of the fine ladies in the gallery and the swaggering gallants stage-side provided inspiration for people to style themselves reflecting individual personality and taste.

A Procession of Actors Arriving in Town (c. 1600). Who could resist attending the performance when they saw the glamorous torch-lit procession of the theatre company in fine costumes, wearing exotic animal masks and carrying intriguing props from their play?!

FURTHER READING

Ashelford, Jane. *A Visual History of Costume: The Sixteenth Century.* BT Batsford, 1983.

Ashelford, Jane. *Dress in the Age of Elizabeth I.* Batsford, 1988.

Cunnington, C. W. and P. E. *Handbook of English Costume in the 16th Century.* Faber & Faber, 1970.

Hatcher, Orie Latham. *A Book for Shakespeare Plays & Pageants.* J. M. Dent & Sons, 1916.

Kelly, F. M. *Shakespearian Costume for Stage & Screen.* A&C Black, 1938.

LaMar, Virginia A. *English Dress in the Age of Shakespeare.* The Folger Shakespeare Library, 1958.

Lawrence, W. J. *The Elizabethan Playhouse & Other Studies.* Shakespeare Head Press, 1913.

Leeds Barroll, J. et al. *The Revels History of Drama in English: Volume III 1576–1613.* Methuen & Co, 1975.

Macquoid, Percy *et al. Shakespeare's England: An Account of the Life and Manners of His Age.* Oxford University Press, 1916.

Norris, Herbert. *Tudor Costume and Fashion.* Dover Publications, 1997.

Picard, Liza. *Elizabeth's London: Everyday Life in Elizabethan London.* Phoenix Paperbacks, 2003.

Rowse, A. L. *The Elizabethan Renaissance: The Life of the Society.* Macmillan, 1971.

PLACES TO VISIT

The Birmingham Shakespeare Library, The Birmingham Library, Centenary Square, Broad Street, Birmingham B1 2ND. Telephone: 0121 242 4242. Website: www.libraryofbirmingham. com (Holds Britain's most important Shakespeare collection, including the Shakespeare Theatrical Gallery and the Shakespeare Memorial Room.)

Fashion Museum, Assembly Rooms, Bennett Street, Bath BA1 2QH. Telephone: 01225 477789. Website: www.fashionmuseum. co.uk (Currently holds the Spence Collection of Elizabethan and Stuart gloves belonging to the Worshipful Company of

Glovers of London, which can also be seen online at www. glovecollectioncatalogue.org.)

Folger Shakespeare Library, 201 East Capitol Street, SE, Washington, DC 20003, USA. Telephone: 001 202 544 4600. Website: www. folger.edu (World-renowned Shakespeare research centre with excellent online resources.)

Gallery of Costume, Platt Hall, Gallery of Costume, Rusholme, Manchester M14 5LL. Telephone: 0161 245 7245. Website: www.manchestergalleries.org (Holds one of the most extensive collections of costume from 1600 to the present.)

Museum of London, 150 London Wall, London EC2Y 5HN. Telephone: 020 7001 9844. Website: www.museumoflondon. org.uk (Holds a vast collection of fashions created and worn in London since the seventeenth century, as well as the Cheapside Hoard, the largest collection of Elizabethan and Stuart jewellery in the world.)

Royal Shakespeare Company, Royal Shakespeare Theatre, Waterside, Stratford-upon-Avon, Warwickshire CV37 6BB. Telephone: 0844 800 1110. Website: www.rsc.org.uk (Regular programme of Shakespeare's plays and exhibitions, including costume exhibits and backstage tours.)

The Shakespeare Birthplace Trust, The Shakespeare Centre, Henley Street, Stratford-upon-Avon, Warwickshire CV37 6QW. Telephone: 01789 204016. Website: www.shakespeare.org.uk (The trust manages all the properties associated with Shakespeare's life in Stratford-upon-Avon as well as the Shakespeare Library Collection and Local History Archive Collection.)

Shakespeare's Globe, 21 New Globe Walk, Bankside, London SE1 9DT. Telephone: 020 7902 1400. Website: www. shakespearesglobe.com (Reconstruction of the original Globe Theatre with regular performances, and library and research facilities.)

Victoria & Albert Museum, Cromwell Road, London SW7 2RL. Telephone: 020 7942 2000. Website: www.vam.ac.uk (World-class collections of costume and textiles, including theatrical costume and theatre and performance galleries.)

INDEX